W9-CCD-890

Komodo Dragons

BY ELIZABETH RAUM

amicus
high interest

Amicus High Interest is an imprint of Amicus
P.O. Box 1329, Mankato, MN 56002
www.amicuspublishing.us

Library of Congress Cataloging-in-Publication Data
Raum, Elizabeth, author.
Komodo dragons / by Elizabeth Raum.
     pages cm.
 Audience: Grades K to grade 3.
 Summary: "Describes Komodo dragons, including what they
look like, where they live, how they hunt, how they reproduce,
and how they fit in the world"– Provided by publisher.
 Includes bibliographical references and index.
 ISBN 978-1-60753-488-4 (library binding) –
 ISBN 978-1-60753-701-4 (ebook)
 1. Komodo dragon–Juvenile literature. I. Title.
 QL666.L29R38 2015
 597.95'968–dc23

                                         2013028242

Editor: Wendy Dieker
Series Designer: Kathleen Petelinsek
Book Designer: Heather Dreisbach
Photo Researcher: Kurtis Kinneman

Photo Credits: Minden Pictures / SuperStock cover; Alex Toso /
Alamy 5; Alexey Senin / Alamy 6-7; Reinhard Dirscherl /
Alamy 9; WaterFrame / Alamy 10; Biosphoto / SuperStock 13;
Biosphoto / SuperStock 14; Roberto Nistri / Alamy 16-17;
Robert King / Alamy 18; Stephen Belcher / Foto Natura /
Minden Pictures / Corbis 21; PHIL NOBLE / Reuters / Corbis
22; Newman Mark / Prisma / SuperStock 25; Nick Young /
Alamy 26; Luca Vaime / Alamy 29

Printed in the United States of America at Corporate Graphics
in North Mankato, Minnesota.

10 9 8 7 6 5 4 3 2 1

Table of Contents

Searching for Food

The Komodo dragon pushes aside tall grass and bushes. His yellow tongue flicks in and out. The tongue picks up scents on the air. The lizard wants to find an animal coming its way. Then he can eat.

Komodo dragons look for animals to eat.

Komodo dragons aren't really dragons. They are broad, thick lizards. In fact, they are the biggest lizards alive today. Males grow up to 10 feet (3 m) long. Females are shorter. The biggest Komodos weigh about 176 pounds (80 kg). They weigh even more after they eat a big meal.

Komodos are as big as grown people.

Komodo dragons live on five small islands. The islands are part of **Indonesia**, a country in Asia. The biggest island is called Komodo. The lizards are named after this island.

Komodo dragons live in forests. They also wander in tall grass. They roam beaches and climb hilly ridges.

Can Komodo dragons swim?

**These islands are home
to Komodo dragons.**

 Yes. They are good swimmers. They swim
from one island to the next.

Komodos swim to a new place.
They keep looking for food.

Dangerous Hunters

Komodos are patient hunters. They wait until the **prey** is about 3 feet (0.9 m) away. That's when the Komodo strikes. It knocks down the prey and bites it. Komodo teeth are large and deadly. They are notched like a saw. When the Komodo bites something, tiny germs called **bacteria** seep into the wound.

Sometimes the prey dies instantly. Other times it dies a few days later of **infection**. Komodos use their tongue to smell the rotting meat. They can smell it up to 1 mile (1.6 km) away. The lizard finds its prey. Then it uses its powerful claws to tear its prey into big chunks.

Why is the Komodo's tongue forked or split?

Flick! Flick! The long tongue can smell food, dead or alive!

A If the smell is stronger on one side, the Komodo goes in that direction to find food.

Two Komodo dragons share a meal.

Q What do Komodos eat?

Komodos live and hunt alone. But the smell of food attracts a crowd. They share the kill. Komodos eat almost everything. They eat bones and hooves. They even eat skin and fur. Komodos are not picky. They eat whatever meat they find. They even eat fish that wash onto the shore.

 They only eat meat. They eat deer and wild boars. Goats and other small mammals make good meals. They even eat small Komodos.

Kings of the Island

Komodo dragons are good hunters. They are the color of clay, so they blend in with the ground. Their prey does not see them coming.

Other animals don't hunt these lizards. The Komodo's powerful tail and sharp claws are no match for them.

Komodos are at the top of the island food chain.

Take a close look at the Komodo's eye. It can see really well.

Komodos have sharp senses that make them excellent hunters. They can see moving objects 985 feet (300 m) away. That's as long as 10 basketball courts.

As they walk, they swing their heads from side to side. This helps their flicking tongues catch scents from all sides. An **organ** in their mouth tells them where they will find their next meal.

Baby Dragons

Komodo dragons **mate** between May and August. There are more males than females. The males wrestle one another for mates. They stand on their hind legs. They use their tails to help them stand. The males grab each other. They push and bite. The loser runs away or lies down.

This Komodo is ready
to fight for a mate.

Baby Komodos hatch from eggs.

Q How big are the babies?

The winner **courts** the female. He flicks his tongue on her snout. He licks her body. If the female agrees, they mate.

In September, the female lays 15 to 30 eggs. The eggs hatch in 8 to 9 months. Some females lie on the nest to protect the eggs. But when the eggs hatch, the female leaves.

 At birth, they are about 6 inches (15 cm) long. They weigh 3.5 ounces (99 g). That's about as much as a cell phone.

Adult Komodos eat babies. The newly hatched babies scramble up trees. It is a safe place. Adults are too big to climb trees. The babies eat insects, eggs, and **geckos**. They grow quickly. By age four, they are 4 feet (1.2 m) long. That's when they leave the trees and begin life on the ground.

Babies live in trees until
they are four years old.

Most of the world's Komodos
live in a park in Indonesia.

Saving Komodos

There are only about 6,000 Komodo dragons in the world. People want to save the lizards. They made the Komodo islands into a national park. The lizards are safe there. People cannot harm or kill them. Many people visit the park. They come from around the world. In 2010, 45,000 people visited the park.

Komodo dragons are dangerous. Their bite can kill humans. Park rangers tell tourists to keep their distance and to be quiet. Rangers do not carry guns. They carry long wooden sticks instead. Rangers push the Komodos away if they get too close. Tourists want to see the world's biggest lizards!

Rangers and guides carry big sticks to keep Komodos away.

Glossary

bacteria Microscopic living things that may cause illness or disease.

court To do special things to try to win a mate.

food chain An ordered arrangement of animals and plants in which each one feeds on the one below it in the chain.

gecko A small lizard that lives in warm places.

Indonesia A country made up of many islands in southeast Asia.

infection A harmful illness caused by germs or bacteria.

mate To come together to produce young.

organ A group of tissues that performs a special task for the body.

prey An animal that is hunted for food.

Read More

Bjorklund, Ruth. *Komodo Dragons.* New York: Children's Press, 2012.

Bodden, Valerie. *Komodo Dragons.* Mankato, Minn.: Creative Education, 2013.

Riehecky, Janet. *Komodo Dragons: On the Hunt.* Mankato, Minn.: Capstone Press, 2009.

Websites

Dragons Are Real!: San Diego Zoo Kids
http://kids.sandiegozoo.org/dragons_are_real

Komodo Dragon: Fort Wayne Children's Zoo
http://kidszoo.org/our-animals/indonesian-rain-forest/komodo-dragon/

Komodo Dragon: National Geographic
http://animals.nationalgeographic.com/animals/reptiles/komodo-dragon/

Index

About the Author

Elizabeth Raum has worked as a teacher, librarian, and writer. She has written dozens of books for young readers. She likes doing research and learning about new topics, and especially enjoyed learning about lizards. Even so, she doesn't want one for a pet! Dogs and cats are cuddlier. Visit her website at: www.elizabethraum.net.